MAKE ME LAUGH!

HORSING AROUND

JOKES TO MAKE EWE SMILE

by Diane L. Burns and Dan Scholten with
Rick and Ann Walton, Joanne E. Bernstein,
Paul Cohen, and Peter and Connie Roop
pictures by Brian Gable

Carolrhoda Books, Inc. • Minneapolis

Q: Which television program shows cow oddities?

A: "Bull-ieve It or Not."

Q: What do you call the ewes on the sidelines of a football field?

A: The shear-leaders.

Q: What do you get when you cross a baby frog with a pig?

A: A polli-hog.

Q: How does a farmer get his hogs to market?

A: In a pig-up truck.

Q: What wind instrument do sheep like to play?

A: The baa-ssoon.

Q: Where do sheep go backpacking?

A: In the wool-derness.

Q: What's a farmer's favorite sport?

A: Fencing.

Q: Why would a little sheep need stitches?

A: If he were bleating.

Q: What has ears but cannot hear?

A: A field of corn.

Q: When is a dog's tail like a farmer's cart?

A: When it's a-waggin'.

Q: What sport do sheep like to play?

A: Baa . . . sketball.

Q: Why do pigs paint themselves green?

A: So they can hide in bushes.

Q: What kind of bushes do pigs hide in?

A: Hambushes.

Q: What kind of pigs hide in hambushes?

A: Hedgehogs.

Q: What did the chicken say when she threw an egg at the farmer?

A: The yolk's on you!

Q: What does a ram say to flatter his mate?

A: "I hear ewe like me."

Q: What do calves eat when they're sick?

A: Chicken moo-dle soup.

Q: Why are sheep so creative?

A: Because they have shear imagination.

Q: What kind of male sheep attracts lots of ewes?

A: A flattering ram.

Q: Why do chickens lay eggs?

A: If they dropped them, the eggs would break!

Q: When is a pig like ink?

A: When it's in a pen.

Q: What's the best way to keep milk from turning sour?

A: Keep it in the cow.

Q: Why is Santa Claus like a farmer?

A: They both like to hoe, hoe, hoe.

Q: Why don't sheep ever get discouraged?

A: They know that where there's a wool, there's a way.

Q: What do you call an unmarried ram?

A: A baa-tchelor.

Q: How much money does a pig have?

A: A pig penny.

Q: Are bulls dignified?

A: Yes, they're always cow-teous and behave in a manner be-hoof-ing a gentleman.

Q: What sheep can jump higher than a tree?

A: Any sheep, because trees can't jump.

Q: What do you get when you cross a pig with an ostrich?

A: A pig who hides her head in the mud.

Q: Why couldn't the farmer's horse run?

A: It was stalled.

Q: What song do rams like to sing?

A: "I Only Have Eyes for Ewe."

Q: What style of clothing do cows wear?

A: Tail-ored.

Q: What do you call sheep who exercise?

A: Wool sweaters.

Q: What's a pig's favorite pet?

A: A hamster.

Q: What did the farmer say when he picked the corn?

A: "Aw, shucks!"

Q: What game is played with a little white ball that goes "b-oink, b-oink, b-oink"?

A: Pig Pong.

Q: Why don't cows smile?

A: Would you smile if your mother gave you grass for dinner every night?

Q: What do you get when you cross a sheep who cuts hair with a coal mining sheep?

A: Baa Baa black sheep.

Q: What type of munchies do sheep take on camping trips?

A: Fleece-dried food.

Q: Where do you clean a dirty hog?

A: At a hogwash.

Q: Where does a sheep go to get clean?

A: The baa . . . th tub.

Q: What made the vegetable farmer so rich?

A: His celery was high.

Q: Who turned the milk cow into a beautiful princess?

A: Her dairy godmother.

Q: Why isn't it much fun to play basketball with a pig?

A: Because he's a ball hog.

Q: Which cow baseball player holds the most milk?

A: The pitcher.

Q: What fish do ewes like to eat?

A: Baa . . . ss!

Q: Why did the farmer let his pigs loose in the woods?

A: He wanted them to go hog wild!

Q: If you find cows in the bullpen, where do you find sheep?

A: In the bleat-chers.

Q: What do pigs put around their yards?
A: Pig-et fences.

Q: In which movie did Dorothy meet the Scare-cow?
A: The Wizard of Ox.

Q: Who is the strongest sheep in the world?
A: Hydraulic Ram.

Q: What's the best way to ride a pig?
A: Piggyback, of course.

Q: What's a cow's favorite food?
A: Cow chow.

Q: What do you get when you cross a sheep with a singing insect?
A: A baa humbug.

Q: Do pigs like to wear shoes?
A: No, they would rather go boar-foot.

Q: What do good little pigs do when they come home from school?

A: Their ham-work.

Q: What do you call a sheep who gives encouragement and support?

A: A wool comforter.

Q: Why are goats so funny?

A: Because they're always kidding around.

Q: Where do cows eat lunch?
A: At the calf-eteria.

Q: What kind of sheep work in the woods?
A: Lamber-jacks.

Q: What do pigs do on Saturday afternoons?
A: Go on pig-nics.

First Farmer: I made a scarecrow so terrible it scared every single crow off my farm.

Second Farmer: That's nothing. My scarecrow is so awful that the crows brought back the corn they stole last year!

Q: Do cows like riddles?

A: Yes, they find them a-moo-sing. (But oxen like yokes.)

Q: How are trees and sheep different?

A: One has limbs. The other has lambs!

Q: What does Smokey the Boar do for a living?

A: He's a Pork Ranger.

Q: What do you call a funny horse?

A: A silly filly.

Q: Why did the farmer plant eggs?

A: He wanted to grow eggplant.

Q: What tree is a sheep's favorite?

A: The weeping wool-ow.

Q: What does a farmer plow but never plant?

A: Snow.

Q: What animals do you bring to bed?

A: Your calves.

Q: What do you call a cow fad?

A: The latest graze.

Q: When does a bull charge?

A: When something Angus him.

Q: What happened to the lost cattle?

A: Nobody's herd.

Q: What does a farmer get when his cows eat peanuts?

A: Peanut butter.

Q: Why did the horse have trouble sleeping?

A: She kept having nightmares.

Q: What kind of pig should you be careful of in a crowd?

A: A pig-pocket.

Q: Which karate move is practiced by every sheep?

A: The lamb chop.

Q: Where do pigs go for excitement?

A: New Pork City.

Q: Where do the pigs in New Pork City go for walks?

A: In Central Pork.

Q: Where do rich New Pork City pigs live?

A: On Pork Avenue.

Q: Where do European pigs live?

A: In Pork-tugal.

Q: Who represents the United States in Pork-tugal?

A: The Ham-bassador.

Q: What do you call the Pork-tuguese pigs when they move to the United States?

A: Immi-grunts.

Q: Which cows get into college?

A: Only the cream of the crop.

Q: What does a sheep go sliding on in the winter?

A: A to-baa-gan.

First Pig: It sure is hot!

Second Pig: I know. I'm bacon!

Q: What does a cow do when someone insults her?

A: She goes off in a hoof.

Q: What do grouchy rams say at Christmastime?

A: "Baaa! Humbug!"

Q: Why is a wild horse so rich?

A: Because he has lots of bucks.

Q: What do sheep like to eat for lunch?

A: Baa-loney sandwiches.

Q: Why don't pigs have fur coats?

A: Because they can't afford to buy them.

Q: Why was the farmer so famous?

A: He was outstanding in his field.

Q: Are sheep much fun to be with?

A: Yes, they are a shear delight.

Q: What kind of music do young sheep listen to?

A: Flock-and-roll.

Q: Where do cow football games take place?

A: In the steer-dium.

Q: Why do cows run in herds?

A: So they can get their sneakers wholesale.

Q: What did Julius Caesar's pet pig speak?
A: Pig Latin.

Q: What do you call an inexpensive chick?
A: A cheap cheep!

Q: What do you get when you cross a pig with a fish?
A: A boar-racuda.

Q: Why are sheep always laughing?
A: Because they are always lambing it up!

Q: What's a pig's favorite city?

A: Piggsburgh, Pen-sylvania.

Q: What kind of bird can eat a barn in one bite?

A: A barn swallow.

Q: What's the difference between a schoolboy studying and a farmer watching his cattle?

A: One is stocking his mind, and the other is minding his stock.

Q: How do baby lambs drink milk?

A: From a baa-ttle.

Q: What does a sheep put on its hooves in the winter?

A: Muttons.

Q: What happened to the pig who got hit on the head with a rock?

A: She got ham-nesia.

Q: Why didn't the horse eat more hay?

A: He still had a bit in his mouth.

Q: How did the first cows come to America on the Moo-flower?

A: In steerage.

Q: Why did the farmer ride his horse to town?

A: It was too heavy to carry.

Q: What kinds of keys won't unlock doors?

A: Donkeys and turkeys.

Q: What cold drink do young sheep sell on hot days?

A: Lamb-onade.

Q: How much do really dirty pigs have?

A: A scent.

Q: How many cows live on this earth?

A: Bullions.

Q: What is in the middle of the cows' football game?

A: Hoof-time.

Q: Where does a farmer keep his young corn?

A: In a corn crib!

Q: What do Hawaiian cows wear?

A: Moo-moos.

Q: What do you call a pony with a sore throat?

A: A hoarse horse.

Q: Where do Russian cows live?

A: Moo-scow.

Q: What sits at your door and oinks at strangers?

A: A watch-pig.

Q: What do you say to a good-looking sheep?

A: "Ewe look marvelous."

Q: Why didn't the farmer tell secrets in his field?

A: Because the corn had ears.

Q: Why don't the people in Sweden export cattle?

A: Because they want to keep their Stockholm.

Q: Do lambs have good manners?

A: Yes, they say "Fleece"and "Thank ewe."

Q: Where do pigs keep their money?

A: In a piggy bank.

Q: What do sheep like to think of as their favorite ancestor?

A: The ewe-nicorn.

Q: Why was the farmer's horse so lucky?

A: Because it had four horseshoes!

Q: How do cattle defend themselves?

A: They know cow-a-ti.

Q: What do lambs like to eat the most?

A: Candy baas.

Q: What do you call a sleeping bull?

A: A bulldozer.

Q: What must cattle remember to bring to camp?

A: Their cow-meras.

Q: What kind of candy do ewes like to eat?

A: Baa-n bons.

Q: What do cows say when they play hide-and-seek?

A: "Leather or not, here I come."

Q: What constellation looks like a pig?

A: The Pig Dipper.

Q: Why was the chicken always in trouble?

A: It used fowl language.

Q: Who delivers little cow babies?

A: The steer-k.

Q: Who puts out fires and rolls in the mud?

A: Smokey the Boar.

Q: What does the watch-pig watch out for most?

A: Ham-burglars.

Q: What do you call a skinny horse?

A: A bony pony.

Q: What fairy tale do lambs like to listen to most?

A: Goldi-flocks and the Three Bears.

Q: What do cows put on their hamburgers?

A: Moo-stard and cow-chup.

Q: What is the bulls' favorite game?

A: Cowhide-and-seek.

Q: Where do rams go to school?

A: At ewe-niversities.

Q: How does a cow do its math?

A: With a cow-culator!

Q: Where do pigs speak Spanish?

A: In Sows America.

Q: What did the cow wear to the football game?

A: A Jersey.

Q: What bluegrass instrument do sheep like to play?

A: The baa-njo.

This book is available in two editions:
Library binding by Carolrhoda Books, Inc.,
  a division of Lerner Publishing Group
Soft cover by First Avenue Editions,
  an imprint of Lerner Publishing Group
241 First Avenue North
Minneapolis, MN 55401 U.S.A.

Website address: www.carolrhodabooks.com

Library of Congress Cataloging-in-Publication Data

    Horsing around : jokes to make ewe smile / by Diane L. Burns . . . [et al.] ;
pictures by Brian Gable.
      p.   cm. — (Make me laugh!)
    Summary: A collection of jokes about farm animals.
    ISBN: 1–57505–662–3 (lib. bdg. : alk. paper)
    ISBN: 1–57505–737–9 (pbk. : alk. paper)
    1. Animals—Juvenile humor. 2. Wit and humor, Juvenile. [1. Animals—Humor.
2. Jokes. 3. Riddles.] I. Burns, Diane L. II. Gable, Brian, 1949– ill. III. Series.
PN6231.A5H67 2005
818'.60208—dc22   2003019357

Manufactured in the United States of America
1 2 3 4 5 6 – DP – 10 09 08 07 06 05